Praise for WORTH BURNING

The poems of Mickie Kennedy's **Worth Burning** are harrowing, authentic, and brilliantly attuned to the deeply observed image. Their flight path is that of a queer coming-of-age at a time when sex was synonymous with death, and a parallel portrait of the artist, for whom poetry is the portal to an expansive erotic imagination. We meet the speaker as "the perfect husband— / grilling brats in the backyard" in an inconvenient marriage of mutual convenience. He then takes us back to childhood and adolescence, and a family whose complex abuses drag him to the brink of self-destruction. What saves him, allegorically, is the "plywood perch" he cobbles in the branches of a pecan tree, a place that "smelled like soil, / like locker room funk." It is the place of witness and self-discovery that some have the guts, ingenuity, and luck to build from the rubble—in other words, poetry. Kennedy's epic tale burns through these exquisitely crafted poems. **Worth Burning** is worth everything.

—DIANE SEUSS, author of **Modern Poetry** and ***frank: sonnets***, winner of the Pulitzer Prize

Worth Burning is riveting and unfailingly honest. As a queer text, a fearless variation on "American Gothic," it's consistently frank and cogent in its episodic delivery of family secrets, desires, and transgressions. In detailing the speaker's progress from bullying and abuse to empathy, commitment, and same-sex joy, these searing, X-ray poems puncture the family romance in breathtaking fashion. Mickie Kennedy is a brave and remarkable new poet.

—CYRUS CASSELLS, 2021 Texas Poet Laureate and author of ***Everything in Life is Resurrection: Selected Poems***

In poems both lavish and hard-edged, Mickie Kennedy explores the stark beauties and startling betrayals of family. His arresting debut, **Worth Burning**, is unapologetic, life-affirming. Attuned to psychology and with a brilliant ear for zany detail, Kennedy is a masterful storyteller-in-verse, balancing the erotic and the everyday, the hilarious and the devastating. No recent book of poems has more lushly and precisely rendered a world and the difficult and wonderful people who make it real.

—RICHIE HOFMANN, author of
The Bronze Arms and ***A Hundred Lovers***

Mickie Kennedy's capacious poetry collection **Worth Burning** journeys from silence and loss toward openness and desire. Brave and honest in its rendering, precise in its concision and imagery, the collection is sure and intimate in its retelling. "I want my life to fit inside my life," reveals the speaker. Brilliant, triumphant, tender, and transcendent, this is a collection that brings together the complexities of the many lives that make up a single life.

—CATHY LINH CHE, author of ***Becoming Ghost***

Worth Burning
poems by Mickie Kennedy

BLACK LAWRENCE PRESS

Executive Editor: Diane Goettel
Book Cover Design: Zoe Norvell
Cover Art: "Smoking" by Steve Binetti
Book Interior Design: Serena Solin

Copyright © Mickie Kennedy 2026

ISBN: 9781625571816

All rights reserved. Except for brief quotations in critical articles or reviews, no part of this book may be reproduced in any manner without previous written permission from the publisher. editors@blacklawrencepress.com

Without in any way limiting the author's exclusive rights under copyright, any use of this publication to "train" generative artificial intelligence (AI) technologies to generate text is expressly prohibited. The author reserves all rights to license uses of this work for generative AI training and development of machine learning language models.

Published 2026 by Black Lawrence Press.
Printed in the United States.

Contents

∞

The Pact ... 13
Beetle Graveyard ... 14
Sheraton by the Airport ... 15
Oasis ... 17
No Leaks ... 18
Having It ... 19
Grimace ... 21
Turning the Key ... 22
Rewiring the Chandelier ... 24
Small Bother ... 25
The Pecan Tree Leaning Away from My Childhood Home ... 26
Obedience Training ... 27
Open Secret ... 28
The Violent Games ... 29
The Gamble, 1992 ... 31
Accidental Wren ... 32
Breach: A Play in Three Parts ... 33

∞

Mouth of Many Endings (I) ... 41

∞

As you might assume from heaven's quiet ... 45
Worth Burning ... 46
Fable ... 48
Accident, 1982 ... 49
Gaps Between the Gaps ... 50
Double-Portrait ... 51
Overstuffed ... 53
Maysville, NC ... 54
American Porn ... 55

Barnfall ... 57
Accidents ... 58
Aiming for Roses ... 59
Bullets in a Work Boot ... 60
Her Business ... 61
Until We Saw Our Faces ... 62
The Night She Stopped Drinking ... 64
Blocked ... 65

∞

Mouth of Many Endings (II) ... 69

∞

Important Things ... 73
Late Arrival ... 74
Aubade with Peaches, Eggs, and Hissing Garlic ... 75
Randy Moves Me Out of Cindy's House ... 76
Out|comes ... 77
Randy Meets My Mom ... 79
Disintegrating Sonnet ... 80
Still Life with Vanna White ... 81
Snapshot of a Girl Refusing to Smile, 1956 ... 83
Rods and Cones ... 84
Breadmaking ... 85
Painted Lady ... 86
Smithfield Valley ... 87
Aubade Where Nobody Leaves ... 88

Notes ... 92
Acknowledgements ... 95

for Randy, Cindy, Meara, and Rowan

The Pact

I feared AIDS, and Cindy feared
being alone, so we forged a compromise.

I cooked, she cleaned, we watched movies
from Blockbuster and read poetry to each other.
On occasion, we coaxed orgasms

with our mouths and hands, never fucking.
She couldn't: a birth defect, chronic vaginismus.
Three years in, she started wanting

kids, and I still wanted what she wanted.
We spent a year with dilators and technicians,
electrodes pulsing her muscles three times a week.
When she was finally ready,

I couldn't dredge up the desire.
We started fighting. Long shouting matches
triggered by everything and nothing.

A twisted miracle: the fighting made me
hard, so we hurried upstairs and fucked.

We fought, we fucked, and out came a daughter.
We fought, we fucked, and out came a son.

Beetle Graveyard

To neighbors, I was the perfect husband—
grilling brats in the backyard, tossing
my kids into the swimming pool,
rubbing sunscreen on Cindy's back.

Pride meant yard work was never finished.
Each shrub tidy as a freshly buzzed head.
Rose bushes to save, their leaves
nibbled ragged by metallic-green

beetles the size of thumbnails.
I set out traps, funnel-topped bags hanging
from branches, each baited
with pheromones. I watched them swell

with dozens, then hundreds, of bodies.
The bags pulsed, almost muscular,
then grew still, rattled only
by a rough breeze. I emptied them out

past my property line, coppery
husks at my feet while the roses
gleamed, aggressively healthy.

Sheraton by the Airport

Face down, blindfolded, propped
on two pillows. The door wedged open
with an empty ice bucket.

He enters.
The clank of a loosened belt buckle.
The soft thud of shoes being tossed aside.
He's the guy who edges my lawn,
who strips to his shorts,
who I watch through a slat in my blinds.

I'm a wisp,
a wasp,
an archipelago.
He's a horse fly,
a portico,
a splitting particle.

His knees on the mattress,
a physical gravity.
He's the guy who bit my thigh
and left a bruise. He's the first man
who ever made me cry.

He drives himself deeper—
a warm, interior blush—as if he might
slam his way through me,
like the biker who
smeared me in engine grease.

He slides away, undone,

already in the bathroom
running water, nearly gone,

but I want him
to touch my cheek and rip
my blindfold off, so he can stop
being everyone
and no one.

Oasis

Outside Vegas, car refueled.
Cindy taps her pink nails
on the plastic glovebox.
A pair of ragged palm trees

looming over a phone booth.
In the restroom, a man
unfastens his overalls,
no divider between us.

He pisses loud, full throttle, a mist
of drops against his legs.
He tucks himself and exits, hands
unwashed. I'm too hard
                              to leave.
Cindy must be wilting in the sun.

No Leaks

I parked in the garage of an abandoned house,
ran a garden hose from my exhaust,

strips of duct tape sealing it shut.
I'd like to tell you I changed

my mind, but the truth—
a realtor dropped by to check out the property.

At the hospital, I learned to paint butterflies.
I watched the anorexics pick at their meals.

A man who never talked
said the staff had stolen his pants.

Why are you sad? my therapist asked.
Because I've always been

my mother's son: a suicide
on low simmer.

Having It

Landline pressing hard
against her cheek. The plastic
stamps her skin. *It hurts,*

she says. *Everything
hurts.* She's gripping her swollen
stomach, a kettle

of green tea gone cold
on the stove. Out back, half-grown
heads of tobacco.

*

The nurse, soft—*He's not
that kind of doctor.* She smiles,
then squeezes her hand.

*

Slumped in an alley,
on break, she lights a Salem
Gold, hesitates. She

has lost all sense of
good, bad. In, out. Self, other
self. She takes a drag.

*

A visit from her
mother. She's holding a home-
made quilt. *For your first-*

born, she says, smoothing
the seams. *You can have it when
you have the baby.*

    *

She jolts from a dream
craving salt. For weeks, honeyed
pork rinds, the only

thing she can eat. Greased
fingertips, sun-varnished days
spent in bed, nauseous.

In the bath, she taps
the bowl of her belly. *My
little carnivore,*

she calls him. A name
is more than a name—omen,
casket, basement, cage.

Grimace

I liked him because nobody knew what he was. We were alike, bulging in all the wrong places. We tottered around, as if our bodies weren't meant for movement. As if our bodies weren't quite ours.

When I was twelve, my mother dropped me at the mall for a meet-and-greet. Grimace was planted in front of a plastic date palm. I was the oldest kid there. Mothers kept shooting me looks. A group of boys pointed, then giggled.

When I reached the front, he was bigger than I imagined—a swollen spade, a hill-sized bruise. He pulled me close for a photo, and I kept myself against his hide, too long. The mothers whispered. *You gotta move on, kid*, said the head inside the head. A soft voice. Too soft. Human.

Turning the Key

An olive-green couch, elbows
almost touching. On the screen: MTV,
Open Your Heart, a dozen men

in claustrophobic rooms, cataloging
every move Madonna made—
a long, muscled leg shooting out

from a chair, a boyish head
of bleached blond hair, the same cut
as Scott's. He knew I was gay.

Everyone did, my voice as soft
as corn silk caught on a bit of barbed wire.
Still, when my hand brushed the edge

of his knee, he didn't move away—
not until the door rattled open.
We scuttled apart. Changed

the channel to something with cops.
A man—red-faced, wiry, gripping
a greasy fast-food bag—appeared

in the doorway. *What did I tell you
about guests?* His voice a rasp. His sour smell
just like my mother's. *Get out,*

Scott said, and I did what I was told.
Crouched on their oil-spattered driveway,
I could hear everything

passing through those plaster walls—
serrated voices, the tinny jingle
of a belt buckle. I stayed right there,

small as I could make myself,
waiting for the screech
of my grandmother's brakes.

Rewiring the Chandelier

Dad was standing on a ladder, his arm lost
in crystal. When the chain snapped,
the chandelier plummeted with him.

He lay there, covered in shattered light.
They tweezed the crystal
from his wounds, took off his boots,

then washed his feet with saline—
the yellow pan turning red.
The doctor said they needed to remove

his little toe, a dangling comma.
I asked my mom if we could keep it,
imagining the toe in our freezer, purple

in a frosty jar. I wanted part of him
entirely to myself. I already knew
I would need a relic.

Small Bother

She was always gentle,
my drunk mother rubbing

her crotch against mine,
as if she were brushing

my hair, or folding
blueberries into batter.

She'd rock herself,
roll over, and pass out.

She never took off her underwear
or my pajamas. I never

reacted, still as a G.I. Joe.
I didn't tell anyone.

It was one small thing
I thought I could handle.

The Pecan Tree Leaning Away from My Childhood Home

I sutured slats of wood to the trunk
and called them stairs. Midway up,
a thick split of branches, ripe

for the plywood perch I cobbled together
with scavenged nails. I felt exposed,
but I could see everything—

two male jays nipping at the almost-ready
ears of corn, my mother at the window
flicking ash, a possum in the burn barrel

searching for a curl of singed potato.
All summer long, the tree dripped sap
on my mother's silver Buick,

and for ten dollars a week, I scoured
those spots with Dad's old undershirts.
Before he died, he said the tree was older

than the house. Older than all of us
combined. It smelled like soil,
like locker room funk, and beneath

each flake of bark, a seething gloss
of ladybugs—dotted, arterial.
Some nights, alone on my perch, I lowered

my shorts. Hoarse cicadas, the lemon smell
of just-cut grass, Jessi Colter love songs
slurring from my mother's bedroom.

Obedience Training

Sultry, smooth as a vulture-picked femur,
it arrived. A boy
at baseball practice lifting his shirt,

exposing his stomach. *Run to him,*
it urged. *Drop to your knees
and adjust his cup.*

Athletes stalked the halls in flimsy tanks—
biceps, deltoids, traps.
Whenever I caught sight of a sweaty pit,

it growled: *Nuzzle! Nuzzle!*
At home, slick with lotion, I let it control
my fantasies. Scott the jock nibbling

my nipples. Petey the pitcher shooting
screw balls down my throat.
Shove a finger in your ass, it said. And I did,

and gasped, it felt so good. *Good,*
it soothed. *You're almost
there. A full-blown queer. My dirty armadillo.*

Open Secret

Mom ignored my black eye,
opened the letter from the principal—
two-day home suspension.

The next day at the mall,
a spindly woman outside Dairy Queen
offered me nuggets speared on toothpicks.
She lowered the plate, said I could take two.

She didn't ask about my eye.
I bet she thinks I gave it to you, Mom said,
dragging a tater tot through ketchup.

After lunch, she handed me five quarters
as she walked inside J.C. Penney.
Don't play the violent games,
she said, *I'll know.*

The Violent Games

The soft flex of the Atari joystick,
button-click, losing
      my body for hours.
The TV greening my skin
         till I heard Mom scratching

at the keyhole. Trickling
down the screen, a pixelated centipede's
      obliterated bits. I wanted
a body like that—battered
         smaller, each piece of me

alive, complete, my city
of selves. The boys
      I craved at lunch,
tables away. Rectangular
         pizzas. Wet willies. The blimp

of my heart in my throat.
Strapped to my chubby wrist,
      a grayscale Pac-Man wristwatch
passed around the cafeteria.
         A circle with a mouth.

Blinking ghosts. They wanted
what I had, which was close
      to being wanted.
In the Skate World arcade,
         a cluster of high school boys

their faces so close

to the Street Fighter screen
        it looked like they wanted to kiss
Ryu, Akuma, Ken, Sagat—
                those hand-drawn muscle-gods

too perfect to be real.
I loomed behind them,
        feet trapped in rental skates,
waist jammed in Toughskin jeans,
                watching the relentless mash

of their fingers. They played
hard, swarming
        the machine, beautiful
fighters spewing 8-bit blood.
                All night long, my fists—

heavy with tokens.

The Gamble, 1992

I followed him down an alley that smelled like piss
and falafel, into an incense-cluttered studio.
I was at my thinnest, my jeans
at their tightest. He wore nothing

but a Duran Duran t-shirt, tight around the shoulders.
A calendar nailed to the wall—
July, a naked cowboy.

Blow jobs were low risk.
We took turns: gentle, hesitant,
too nervous to shoot.

I kept his number, a landline,
and kept coming back. Roasted chicken,
rosemary, white wine in a water glass, his hand
on my crotch as he confessed

that he nearly became a priest
before finding his true calling—fingers
on the elastic rim of my boxers.

Because we were in love,
and because we'd been tested, I let him
fuck me—our bodies a crisp sheet
snapping in the wind. We were safe.
We thought we were safe.

Accidental Wren

Stars collect
in the colander of night.
Children tucked in.
Curtains drawn tight.

*

A flock rises
as wind ruffles
into a singular
nothingness.

*

Inside the camera's eye,
lodged somewhere
between griefs,
the photo not taken.

*

We could never
through the evening
fill the screen
with anything but this.

*

A priest rides a horse
near a stream.
For thirty years,
no word for mother.

Breach: A Play in Three Parts

Act I, Scene I

Tommy's left hand submerged
in a bucket thick with ice.
A neat, sunlit kitchen.
Minutes pass. He wants
to be numb enough.
With a scalpel he stole
from his father's office,
he shears flat warts
from his fingers. He wants
to be beautiful. Blood
fills the tiny craters.

Act I, Scene II

Tommy and Mickie alone in a walk-up attic.
It looks like they're stepping on eyes,
the floorboards made from knotted pine.
Tommy opens a tin and pours
liquid mercury into the bowl of his hands.
The metal jitters like a body.
The wing of an owl sputters from a rafter.

Act I, Scene III

A scatter of car magazines.
A mattress on the floor.
Slightly damp dollar bills

tossed on the sheets. Tommy leans
against the wall. He's dressed
in his mother's satin lingerie,
brassiere sagging with water balloons
he filled with a garden hose.
Mickie stands a foot away, afraid
he'll touch the wrong thing.

Act II, Scene I

Tommy and Mickie alone on a loveseat,
close but not quite touching.
An exposed bulb in a frat basement,
a swaying pull-chain.
In Tommy's lap: a ball point pen,
a strip of aluminum foil, a stolen
lighter, a plastic bottle—a hole
cored through the cap.
Tommy unzips a tiny Ziploc,
and Mickie pretends it's full
of salt, snow, teeth.

Act II, Scene II

Before a housefly settles
on a half-eaten bagel, it visits
a mug, a lamp, a window, a lip.

Act II, Scene III

[A landline screams]

Who is this?
[Silence]
Tommy, is that you? Do you need help?
[Silence]
Are you there?
[Silence]

[A landline screams]

ACT III SCENE I

An email:

*Mickie, car broke down in Tennessee
mountains. Engine went to shit. Mom
in hospital. Lymphoma. It's bad. Need
cash so I can see her. I hate
asking, but you know me.
I'm your Tommy.
Western Union Food City #611.
Pay to: my name.*

ACT III SCENE II

Neon shoving through drawn shades.
The crush of gravel in a motel lot.
Above the bed, off-kilter, a framed giraffe
folding itself in half to drink.
A woman guides Tommy's hand
to her bra strap. She's dressed
in lace, sunspots on her breasts.
The money is gone. The drugs, gone.
She takes his cock inside her mouth.
Tommy mortars shut his eyes.

ACT III SCENE III

A manicured backyard garden.
Mickie teeters at the top of a ladder,

his body wearing an oak
like a condom. His wife
strokes across the pool.
Slowly, calmly, he slides the tip
of his finger inside
a vespid wasp's paper nest.

Mouth of Many Endings (I)

     1

the earth is acute
asphalt along a stretch of leg
     anger rests her axle

the form a mother takes to mother
against the slap a sound
against the moon a cloud
a child from that tree half-bent

     2

suppose the mother supports the phlox
     resists the sleeves
agrees the children out the door

a brick with bad intentions
a heavy crush of bread

     she slumps a box inside me

3

the folding of a letter into sleep
an oath in isolation
a tusk begins to grow a crown of sand

she speaks the tongues they fork
shapes into face
scissors upon the scissors on the dresser

4

ash-blond and unable
a child two dimes awake

a resemblance of embers
the corpses a chorus
       a mother steers the night

As you might assume from heaven's quiet

Mom still lives.
The bracelet I should give her—

a coral snake eating its own tail.
I take her semi-monthly calls,

though I probably shouldn't.
I imagine you, Dad, nose against glass,

breath steaming up to obscure
your face. When you knocked in my dream

I kept you outside.
The photograph of your wedding:

Mom, wide-eyed and startled;
you, drunk and satisfied.

Given the date, I know I was there too,
sipping champagne in utero.

I keep our calls safe,
a fractured shorthand:

the humidity, my kids, the lawn.
She asks when I'm coming to see her,

even though she knows
the answer—I won't be going home

until I'm tucking her into the ground
right next to you.

Worth Burning

Behind our house, Mom shoves
twigs into the burn barrel.
Plastic bottles melt,

turning the smoke green.
Most locals burn their trash;
the dump charges two dollars a bag.

A donut caramelizes
into a small fist,
rotting potato peels curl.

She stirs the rubbish with a long, metal pipe.
Cinders flit in the air like flies.
A loud pop, hiss.

Can of hairspray, she says,
still stirring.
I'll reek of smoke

until I shower, touching myself
to the images stuck
inside my head—

the butcher who always
double-wraps our ground beef;
the man I found,

bald head and hairy back,
on top of my mom
on the living room floor.

She prods the trash, pushing it down
towards the low flames.
There's always a piece, she says,

whacking the side of the barrel.
A goddam piece
that just won't burn.

Fable

A bald eagle landed on a tree
outside my bedroom window and called me
a fruitcake.

I spent a summer with alley cats,
tipping trashcans and torturing mice.

Dad told me Uncle Russell wasn't my uncle,
and wasn't named Russell.

I kissed the high school quarterback
in the locker room,
then devoured a gallon of ice cream.

Mom was so drunk she pissed the couch
and tried to flush the lamp.

I stepped on a frog because I knew
I could bring him back to life,
and I did.

Accident, 1982

My dad was struck by a drunk driver.
Walking home, a paper bag

full of chips and soda, two candy bars
crushed at the bottom. Struck

by a drunk driver, walking home, my dad.

Gaps Between the Gaps

My mother bastes herself
with baby oil and iodine. I peel
a bumper sticker from her dented Buick.

She's not cooking this month. I search
for something to hold. The gaps
between the gaps. My best friend's swimsuit

hanging on a door handle. My brother
scours dishes with the vegetable brush.
I find the sweet spot on the radio.

Mother sweeps into the kitchen. She's wearing
one of Dad's old flannel shirts. No shorts, tan legs.
She grabs the broom and pulls it close,

spinning slow around the cluttered table.

Double-Portrait

    I. Clamming

Grandpa stayed with clams the longest—
hunched at a sink, spraying grit

from the grooved shells.
Little necks, cherry stones,

top necks, chowders: beautiful names
for such hard creatures.

Pips were too small to be sold.
We tossed them into fifty-pound onion bags

and buried them deep in the mud
beneath a sun-scarred pier.

For months, the pips filter-fed,
growing so plump they split the mesh.

Grandpa paid me a nickel for each one
I recovered, wading out alone,

seagulls perched on the pilings.
It felt like the clams wanted me

to wedge them open, releasing
their smell—brine and sweet decay.

II. Matriarch

Grandma couldn't afford
      music. No time for it—climbing
            the grain bin, tightening

belts on the work truck,
      replacing tires taller than her
            on the farm's only tractor.

Once, on New Year's Eve,
      Uncle Russell put Elvis on,
            and Grandma folded—snapping

her fingers, swaying on the shag
      with bare feet while she mouthed
            the words to "Suspicious Minds."

Her sun-toughened skin, her eyes
      the color of wet dirt—all of it
            softened, more fluid than usual.

She grabbed my hands and we danced
      in circles, fireworks skittering.
            Touch was a rare thing between us,

but that night, we weren't
      who we always were. She let me
            lean my head against her dress.

Overstuffed

Each summer, two long weeks, feasting past
the point of hunger. Mostly sweets—

a strawberry Danish, a turnover, a lemon
tart, the distant clang of spoons

lulling me to sleep. We never knew
exactly where my mother went,

but Grandma always marked her return
with a pie—perfectly crimped crust,

steam coiling from the slits.
Mother always came back thinner

than the cigarettes she tapped
against the table. She dissected her piece

with frenetic precision.
I ate so fast it made me sick.

Grandma sat between us, holding
a butter knife, in case we wanted more.

Eating was all she ever asked of us.
For her, I would have eaten myself.

Maysville, NC

That summer, I baled hay for pennies,
twine pulling my fingers raw.
They healed tougher, better.
Late July, I found a snake
writhing inside a bale,
dark as a pulsing vein.
Neighbors up the street
brought plates of Sunday dinner
to the convenience store
where Mom worked—
meatloaf, fried chicken, pot roast.
We ate in the back room on a table
made from wooden Coke crates.
A farmer up the street
came in each week with clean jokes
memorized from *Reader's Digest*.
Once, he invited us to dinner,
country ham and red-eye gravy over rice.
My mother told me not to leave her
alone with him, just in case
he got ideas, which he didn't.
His daughter had a brain injury,
mid-thirties and full of exuberance,
addicted to mysteries
from the Bookmobile. They kept
a pool table in an old converted barn.
All night, the farmer let me win.

American Porn

A scratched VHS, no label.
The good stuff, he said, *first one
is free*. I was fifteen. He knew

what I wanted. My uncle's friend.
I can't remember his name,
but he believed the future

was laserdiscs, an imposing display
on every wall. A patchy beard
hiding acne scars. A lit cigarette,

bouncing. He almost looked
like the man on the tape, Ron Jeremy—
a greasy mullet, lush pubes,

a big belly knocking against
a woman. She was face down,
a formality, as if she wasn't

the reason the tape was made.
For me, it was all Ron, and Ron's buddy
goading him on, off to the side,

chest hair dense as steel wool.
The quality was shit (spider-webbed, copied
to the near point of static) but it was all

we had, me and the boys I lent it to.
I was their librarian, passing
the tape from hand to hand.

I imagined them alone in their rooms,
boxers around their ankles, seeing
what I saw: an undercover cop

kissing a pistol to Ron's temple. A brief
stillness. The pulling out. The woman
unfolding herself from the table,

then kneeling down. The back of her
bobbing head, and Ron's hand reaching
for the cop's shoulder, resting there.

Barnfall

The lock was rusted shut on an abandoned barn.
Ted and I used hammers and pry bars
to tear the door from its hinges. We took

a hatchet to the back wall, made a window
overlooking the acres of corn his parents owned.
They kept their home as rigid as a field.
Reluctantly, each night, we disappeared—

me to my mother's drinking; Ted to his parents'
rancher where, in a detached garage out back,
he hanged himself.
                        After the funeral, I took
a hydraulic car jack to the barn, crushing
each support beam, the stairs and walls.
The bone-crackling sound of wood torn apart.
The squeak of nails pulled from their holes.

Accidents

The dog who had me as a boy,
a collie named Lady,
struck by a van. She dragged herself
onto our porch, panting,
a trickle of blood in each nostril.
Every time I touched her,
she winced. She lingered
until my father arrived,
licking the hand that held the rifle.

*

When I left for college, I left
an indoor cat named Kitty
with my mother,
who banished him outdoors.
A month later, his body
by the curb, a flattened
skull. *He sprinted
towards the wheels*, she lied.

*

The other day, a squirrel streaked
across the road. I braked,
but it jerked back
under the car, unable to place
where the danger was.
The pop beneath my tire almost
joyful—like a baseball
smacking into a mitt.

Aiming for Roses

When the lights in the house flickered then died,
Dad threw a tarp over the clothesline.

Mom forced a smile. *Isn't this fun?* she said.
Camping, but without the bears and brambles.

We ate from the freezer till everything spoiled,
then mostly from cans,
then mostly from nothing.

The hallway phone still worked, a mystery.
Mom stood in that dark hallway for hours,
laughing into the receiver.

Dad taught me to whittle sticks into spears,
how to piss outside—unzipping
in the darkness, a babble of urine.

Your mother's roses, he said, *look thirsty.*

Bullets in a Work Boot

Dad bent briars to the ground with boots
so I could make it to the creek

without tearing my clothes.
Snarled roots in the creekbed's edge,

some of them stranded above the water,
others etching into the flow.

The air was still, respectful.
The current scraped the closed mouths

of ordinary stones. We lured
minnows with our fingers,

his gun propped against a trunk,
not even loaded. He needed

a break—from her, from that house,
but somehow not from me.

This was before he fed me my first
persimmon. Before a fallen tree

would erase a slice of the forest's canopy,
sunlight punching through.

Her Business

There's something inside her, a sentence
wrapping around itself. Her eyes
eight decades deep. She forgets

where she is, where she left
her apple-printed apron, the one she's used for years,
to dry her hands when the phone rings.

Each day, she picks up the receiver
for a dial-tone. The sound of plastic on plastic
as she settles it back in its cradle.

She's begun the business of arranging her end.
One good dress on a hook in the closet.
Uncashed Social Security checks jammed in the mailbox.

For weeks, the lights stutter, then cut completely.
She drops two slices of rye in the toaster,
then takes the toaster out the door, down the hill—

a housedress of a woman in late April.
The smell of lemon dish soap and brown paper bags.
The black cord dragging its line in the dirt.

Until We Saw Our Faces

Mother and son, hunched
in the formal dining room, massaging
        the silver. Our hands

in yellow gloves to keep our skin
        from the sear of the Wright's cream,
which smelled like a pack of quarters

dipped in lemon juice—sharp, dizzying,
like mother's breath when she drank.
        The table was dressed in newspaper.

The shades were up because she wanted
        the neighbors to catch a glimpse
of our elegance: a tea service,

candlesticks, Chantilly silverware
released from a velvet-lined box.
        Mother watched while I swirled

my fist in the gravy boat.
        I was slow, deliberate. Even
the parts she couldn't see

needed to gleam. We rinsed
everything in the clawfoot tub—
        a grainy slough, a stampede

of iridescence. Mother gossiped
        while we buffed each piece
with Dad's old undershirts.

A hushed divorce. A baby
out of wedlock. Every house a house
        of sin, besides our own.

The Night She Stopped Drinking

Rigid at the kitchen table, a plate
of spaghetti gone cold. *I should erase
my little mistake,* she slurred,
a handgun jumping between targets:
first me, then her, then me again.

When she finally passed out, I scattered
the bullets like seeds: buried
in a shoe beneath my bed, inside
a vase, under my pillow—like a tooth
she'd knocked from my head.

Blocked

Three days. Five. I sat so long
my legs grew numb,
but Mom wouldn't let me leave
until I went. She fed me sour
chocolates, a powder that tasted like hay.

She bought a water bottle
topped with a beak-like nozzle.
This will work, she said.
Sluggish, clogged, I prayed
she was right.

In the tub, she stripped me down
and bent me over. *Please
trust me,* she urged, and I felt
a liquid fullness
like I'd pissed myself

inside myself. *Hold it
for a minute*—and I did,
despite the pressure.
Despite my stomach, so loud
it sounded like

it was trying to speak.
Keep holding it, she said,
and I did. And I would,
for years.

Mouth of Many Endings (II)

    1

sent within a field of must
transitive the child cowers

breasts in the static breech of bone
glass textures into aster

a heart among this friction
a head slides days upon the floor

    2

the light behind a lowered certain
       a mother collects a hundred sons

we knew nothing but smell
the receding night
a continent of asterisks

a boa descends the body
       inside me go crawling

3

and so the mother exits
never to ticket the tile with daisies
searching their collars for something to say

      a synapse occurs
the sun removes a tooth

4

did you forget a shovel
how the candle melts itself to sleep

      iron in a chorus of rust
two cogs negotiate a breath

she a brandy to imbibe
closet sideways

a mother marks the water's anger
the child failures into length

Important Things

I cruise the restroom looking for a man
who used to meet me here on Wednesdays—
hairy calves, muddy work boots.
I step into the back stall, turn the lock, wait.

Finally, a bang on my door:
Police. It's time to finish up.
They're always cruising the cruisers.
I flush and leave, walking under his gaze

to the sink. No paper towels.
I wipe my hands on my jeans.

Where had Mr. Wednesday gone?
Back to his wife. Or maybe he moved.

It's been ten years
since the man I almost loved
rested his head on my chest,
expelling a sparrow's worth of breath.

What I would ask him now—
*Will you sit on my childhood porch
and clink bottles of Newcastle Brown?*

We could talk about the important things,
like the best color to paint the chairs.
Or the men we've lost. Or how
I'm finally ready. Not dropping
his hand when the neighbors walk past.

Late Arrival

We stand naked by the window. Long
shadows. The sputter of hooves across
the porch. A doe and newborn fawn
lick salt from the overnight frost,

scraping clean the wooden slats.
I tuck my chin into his shoulder. The wreck
of myself, exposed, pressing against his back.
The doe shivers. The fawn snaps its neck

upright, staring through the single pane of glass.
Beautiful, he says, and it is. I kiss
his cheek, hiding what I know from him:

in April, if I walked the woods
for downed elms or signs of bear, I would
see that fawn again—a scatter of bones.

Aubade with Peaches, Eggs, and Hissing Garlic

In the pre-sun stillness, the kitchen ticks—
                an insect-wing click. Raw sourdough

on the rise. Sliced peaches. A knife
                whispering through a tomato, crushed

basil, a spiced musk mingling
                with last night's touch—his tongue

on the cords of my neck. He lifts
                a slivered peach to my lips. *Call me*

by your name, he jokes, and I don't,
                but I almost do. All my life,

a resistance. A turned face. *Teach me*,
                he says, and I hand him a spoon.

He's always been the teacher—a swish
                in his step from the day he could walk—

but I do my best. I show him how
                to hold his wrist, fold the cream,

mashed garlic spitting in the pan.
                When he stirs, he stirs with his hips,

a private dance he doesn't feel
                the need to hide, or halt. I bend

for the bread. He drizzles honey.
                There's room for both our mouths.

Randy Moves Me Out of Cindy's House

I want all the books, all
the photos on the walls,
even the walls, the ones
I painted the color of straw.
I want the dusty rugs,
the carpets, the subfloor, the slab,
the sinks covered in toothpaste,
skylights, scouring pad,
Dyson ball, Frigidaire,
mixing bowl, salad tongs,
rolling pin, Cindy's pants, the double
toaster, spider plants, corkboard
coasters, the carrot peeler,
Rowan's cleats, the threadbare
sheets, some cheap whiskey,
and Meara's baby teeth.
I want my life to fit inside my life.

Out | comes

    I

Are you the guy or the girl? Mom asks.
Both. Neither. Her hands
malignant swans on the table.

    II

She harpoons a rainbow. Skittle-hail smacks the roof.

    III

She dabs her eyes with her *Love Wins* apron.
Oh Sonny, I love it when you Cher.

    IV

Are you sure? She looks me up and down.
You dress like a Wal-Mart dumpster.

    V

Yes god my precious twinkie slays the house!

VI

She squeezes a cubed steak.
Blood hits a sizzling frying pan.
My little abortion, she says, touching my cheek.

VII

How much? she asks,
opening her checkbook.
*How much to make you
change your mind?*

Randy Meets My Mom

Together on the couch, our knees nearly touch.
Mom looks at us, cocking her head
as she strips the wrapper from a Baby Ruth.
How's Cindy, she asks, *your wife?*

Randy clears his throat. Mine tightens.
Mom adjusts her elastic waistband
as she ambles to the bathroom. Once she's gone,

He drops his hand on mine. I almost shake him
off. The clock releases three brass notes.
My knee bounces. We wait
for the toilet's hushed roar,

staring at a picture on the wall—
a farmer crumpled against a stone barn,
a straw hat covering his eyes.

Disintegrating Sonnet

A dream of a single white cow,
a white crow, the dissolving blues
of memory and magnolia,

the hopeless pebble of the moon.
A jar of activated darkness.
A satchel of glass birds.

A priestess slinks a copper dress
across her temporal cortex.
No one is free.
Not even the trash men. Not even the trash.

The bones of a newly imagined breeze.
The stiletto in my ventricle.
A cloth doll on a crocodile's tongue.
The body has moved on.

Still Life with Vanna White

My mother thinks my brother
               is her husband. One hand crawling

inside an extra-large Hardee's fry,
               the other cuffing his wrist

to the kitchen table. Her mind,
               elsewhere. *Where's little Mickie,*

she snaps, lifting a can of Tab.
               Oh right, she says, *I switched*

his ass and sent him off to bed.
               A beating, four decades old,

back in the kitchen—plastic
               roosters on a crooked shelf,

yellowing newspapers stacked
               where my father used to sit.

Out the window, a blue jay
               bullies its head inside the feeder.

The sigh of a braking school bus.
               Mother hunts a thought, her jaw

flexing, as if she's wrestling
               a sesame seed from her gums.

My brother fiddles with the remote.
                Tinny applause. Pat's hair plugs.

A woman buying a vowel, O.
                The ding of a tile going blue.

Snapshot of a Girl Refusing to Smile, 1956

Behind her hands, she hides
a dirt-smudged face. She's not
wearing her good dress because it's not Sunday
and no one has died. Her world:

tobacco. The guttural cough of a combine
chewing through a nearby field.
It's July, eastern North Carolina.

Swimming in overalls her brother outgrew,
she's waiting for something
to carry her into a glossier life.

She looks feeble, unlike herself,
her fingertips a sickly yellow-green.
That was her job—protecting

the tobacco leaves. Mashing caterpillars.
It's like she was rehearsing
her future: small, hard.

I'm sure she didn't want it.
Being the girl dressed as a boy
hunting hornworms in those tidy rows.

But what we don't want rarely matters.
For example: I never wanted to be her son.
And she never wanted to be so alone,
at the end of it all—queen of a yellowing couch.

Rods and Cones

Randy is colorblind. He never knows
the shades of my son's shirts.
No blues or greens,
everything gray, red, yellow—
like all the cars he's ever owned.

They sell special glasses online,
each designed for a specific color deficiency.
I bought him every pair.

Hands shaking, he tried each one,
willing the blues and greens
to appear. Nothing changed.
A box of failure.

I should've taken him out for mozzarella sticks,
to Gutterball Palace,
the one with spicy marinara—his favorite
red. I should've taken him

into our garden and guided his finger
inside a daffodil's ruffled mouth.
For a few hours, everything he touched
would've worn a smudge

of pollen. A light switch. A roll of paper towels.
His collar. My cheek. Everywhere,
a dusty shadow he could see.

Breadmaking

My son wipes flour onto his pants.
I remind myself I'm not my mother's
anger, lifting him up to the sink
so he can wash his hands.

Water soaks the ends of his sleeves.
The loaf rises, slowly at first,
white and swollen,
like his belly when he sleeps.

He presses his face to the oven's glass.
Yes, he'll leave a smudge,
but I let him stay
because I want to see him see

the edges turning golden.
In the living room, the calico twitches
awake. I place the bread
on the counter, tear off a steaming piece.

He takes it from me, and I'm sure
it's searing his fingers.
Stupid, blessed boy—he doesn't let go.

Painted Lady

My daughter's childhood horse, her coat a color
between caramel and cured tobacco, died

standing up. When she went down,
she took three rails with her.

When a horse dies, there's an entire day
dedicated to the physical body.

A case of beer, a friend and a backhoe
to bury her where she lies.

A clutch of country doves
attended the funeral, as did Cindy.

My daughter stayed in the house.
She had already closed that chapter years ago:

too grown to ride. How long had she gone—
nobody's fingers untangling her mane?

The grave was a mound of red clay.
Cindy scattered wild flowers.

I caught my daughter's face
pressed against her window, a second-story moon.

Later that night, when she thought
she was alone, I watched her drain the trough,

rolling it gently on its side.

Smithfield Valley

Pasta Pete's, weak jazz
spilling from tinny speakers.
In the shadows out front,
two cigarettes glow orange.

Second-class citizens, Mom says.
She's not smoking these days,
though I still find butts in aluminum foil
tucked in a potted plant on her patio.

After dinner, we drive to a hill.
She leans on me as we walk
to an overlook, sun setting, a rash
of red and pink like the clay

in the ditch behind her shed.
From here, our town looks just as small
as it feels: the houses are blocks
a kid could hold, or throw.

This view, she says, *deserves a cigarette,*
rustling through her purse.
I know, I know—they're killing her.
I almost wish they weren't.

Aubade Where Nobody Leaves

My husband's thumb on the edge
of his lip. A tiny pool of spit
darkening his pillow, his mouth

always open. He slips into deep sleep
so damn easily, like a child
who hasn't experienced fear.

A bruised grapefruit from the fridge
cut in half and spiked with sugar. A startle
of sparrows on the elm out front.

Today I am not a ten-year-old boy
hiding from his mother.
I walk the crushed gravel of my driveway,

polyps of dew on the plastic sleeve
protecting the newspaper.
The bullfrogs sound masculine,

a smoker-cough chorus.
I can see my neighbor on her knees,
a silver spoon in her hand.

She's digging at the roots of weeds,
loosening the soil.
It looks like she's eating the earth.

Beyond her, more houses—
plaster walls containing rooms,
rooms containing bodies, bodies

containing everything
we are, and were. A mangy rabbit
streaking across the lawn.

Purple cabbage in the front flower bed.
A grown man walking back inside
to nudge another man awake.

Notes

"Beetle Graveyard" (14): this poem was inspired by Benjamin S. Grossberg's poem, "Beetle Orgy."

"Having It" (19): this poem, which is composed of haiku stanzas, owes its form to Emily Leithauser's poem, "Haiku for a Divorce."

"Turning the Key" (22): this poem references Madonna's "Open Your Heart" music video, which was directed by Jean-Baptiste Mondino.

"Accidental Wren" (32): the lines "Stars collect / in the colander of night" were inspired by Dorianne Laux's poem, "My Mother's Colander."

"American Porn" (55): the adult movie referenced is *Amanda by Night* (1981), directed by Gary Graver, starring "Veronica Hart" and "Ron Jeremy."

"Aubade with Peaches, Eggs, and Hissing Garlic" (75): this poem references the 2017 movie *Call Me By Your Name*, directed by Luca Guadagnino, which was based on the 2007 novel of the same name by André Aciman.

Acknowledgements

Gratitude to the editors and journals that housed earlier versions of these poems:

Adroit: "The Pecan Tree Leaning Away From My Childhood Home"
Allium: "Matriarch," "Sheraton by the Airport"
Assaracus: "Breach, A Play in Three Parts"
Brawl Lit: "Aiming for Roses," "The Night She Stopped Drinking"
Colorado Review: "Clamming," "Maysville, NC"
Copper Nickel: "Worth Burning"
Electric Lit's The Commuter: "Out|comes," "Smithfield Valley"
Fairy Tale Review: "Overstuffed"
Gulf Coast: "Fable"
Hobart: "Obedience Training"
Hunger Mountain: "As you might assume from heaven's quiet"
Ilanot Review: "Small Bother," "The Pact" previously titled "The Pact, 1994"
Indiana Review: "Still Life with Vanna White"
Indianapolis Review: "Important Things," "Randy Meets My Mom"
Little Patuxent Review: "Bullets in a Work Boot" previously titled "Squirrel Hunting"
New Ohio Review: "Grimace"
Nimrod: "Barnfall," "Painted Lady," "Rewiring the Chandelier," "Rods and Cones,"
"The Gamble, 1992"
Ninth Letter: "Aubade Where Nobody Leaves"
Pirene's Fountain: "Gaps Between the Gaps"

Prairie Schooner: "The Violent Games" and "Until We Saw Our Faces"
PRISM International: "Randy Moves Me Out of Cindy's House" previously titled "My New Husband Moves Me Out of My Wife's House"
Salt Hill: "Snapshot of a Girl Refusing to Smile, 1956" previously titled "Portrait With Pall Malls"
Sixth Finch: "Open Secret"
Shō Poetry Journal: "American Porn" previously titled "American Porn, 1985"
South Carolina Review: "No Leaks"
Tampa Review: "Breadmaking"
The Pinch: "Disintegrating Sonnet"
Typishly: "Her Business" previously titled "Unraveling"

For their invaluable feedback on this book during its development, my gratitude extends to Josh Tvrdy, Susan Tichy, Diane Seuss, Richie Hoffman, Benjamin Grossberg, David Trinidad, Randall Mann, Carolyn Forché, Dorianne Laux, Elizabeth Knapp, Eduardo Corral, Cyrus Cassells, Eileen Myles, Lise Goett, Jeffrey Levine, Stephen Mills, and the members of the Slant Light poetry group: William Derge, Nichole Dowlearn, Deb Sinek, James Hopkins, and Wayne Drozynski.

I'd like to extend special thanks to many teachers and friends, some of whom are no longer with us, who have supported my writing over the years: McKay Sundwall, Patrick Bizzaro, Michael Hamer, Peter Makuck, Julie Fay, David Sanders, Peter Klappert, Richard Bausch, Judy Marshall, Louisa Ringo, Joyce Herring, Tommy Turlington, Tom McAllister, Fran Kenney, Jennifer Hanes, Allison McAlister, Dave Seldon, Andrew Cotterman, and Wade Turlington.

MICKIE KENNEDY is a gay writer who resides in Baltimore County, Maryland. His work has appeared in *POETRY*, *The Threepenny Review*, *The Southern Review*, *The Sun* and elsewhere. His work explores queerness, family, illness, and survival. When not writing, he runs eReleases, a press release distribution company. Follow him on social media @MickiePoet or his website mickiekennedy.com.

www.ingramcontent.com/pod-product-compliance
Lightning Source LLC
Chambersburg PA
CBHW060537080526
44586CB00012B/772